The
Classic Wedding
Collection

ISBN 1-57560-256-3

Cover photo by Eric Naaman

Visit our website at www.cherrylane.com

The Classic Wedding Collection

Prelude Music

Processional Music

Interlude Music

Recessional Music

Postlude Music

Air

Wolfgang Amadeus Mozart

Canon In D

Johann Pachelbel

Air
from *Water Music Suite*

George Frideric Handel

Air On A G String

Johann Sebastian Bach

Chorale

from *Anna Magdalena Notebook*

Johann Sebastian Bach

Jesu, Joy Of Man's Desiring

Johann Sebastian Bach

Andante cantabile

Elegie

Jules Massenet

dim. e rit.

Minuet

from *Anna Magdalena Notebook*

Johann Sebastian Bach

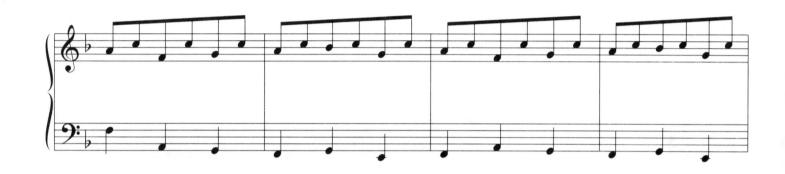

Minuets I & II

Henry Purcell

MINUET I

Allegretto

MINUET II

Sleepers, Wake*

Johann Sebastian Bach

*May be used as prelude or interlude music.

Theme From Romeo And Juliet

Peter Il'yich Tschaikovsky

Andante cantabile

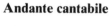

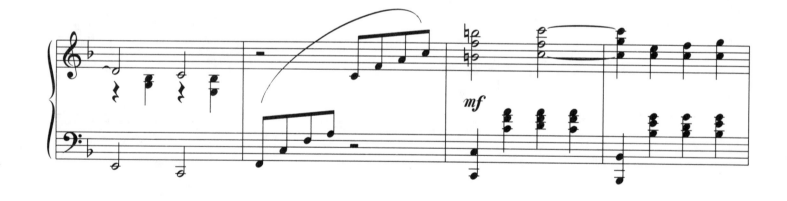

cresc. poco a poco

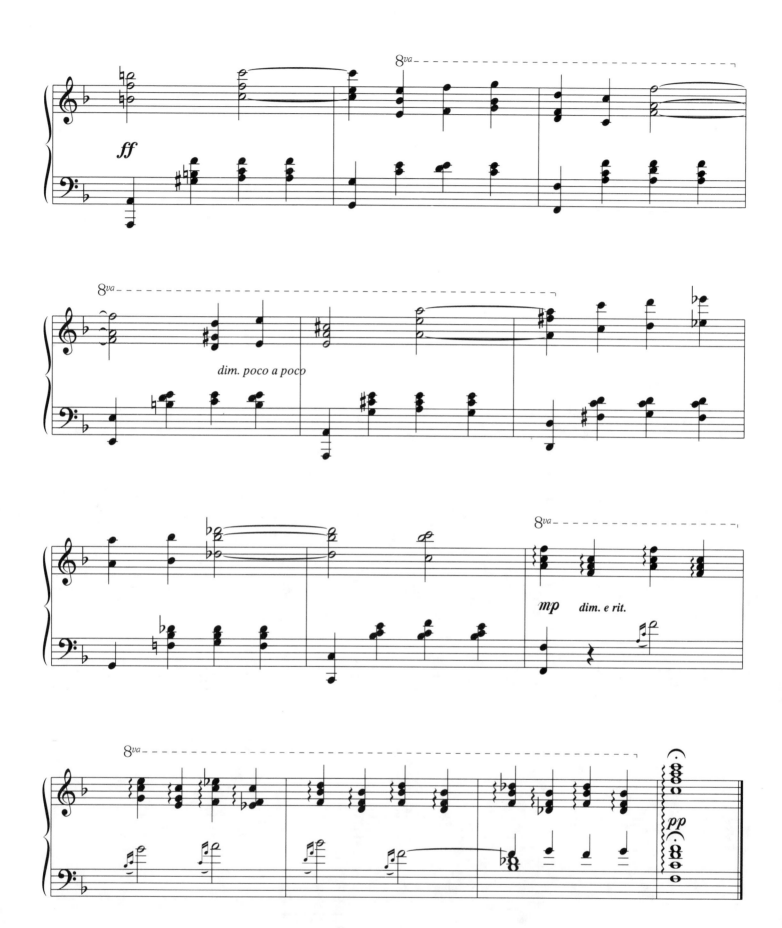

Allegro Maestoso

George Frideric Handel

Allegretto

Bridal Chorus

from *Lohengrin*

Richard Wagner

March

George Frideric Handel

Prince Of Denmark's March

Jeremiah Clarke

Processional

from *Royal Fireworks Music*

George Frideric Handel

Processional

from *St. Anthony Chorale*

Franz Joseph Haydn

Processional

from *Water Music Suite*

George Frideric Handel

Trumpet Tune

Jeremiah Clarke

Allegro moderato

Adagio

Alessandro Marcello
trans. by Johann Sebastian Bach

Be Thou With Me

(Bist Du Bei Mir)

Johann Sebastian Bach

soul shall rest in deep re - pose. My heart is glad
Ster - ben und zu mei - ner Ruh' Ach, wie is ver - gnügt

When thou art near me, My eye - lids closed by thy ten - der
wär' so mein En - de, Es drück - ten dei - ne schö - nen

hands, My eyes with love will rest on thee. My heart is
Hän - de mir die ge - treu - en Au - gen .zu. Ach, wie ver -

glad When thou art near me, My eye - lids
gnügt wär' so mein En - de, Es drück - ten

44

closed by thy——— ten - der hands,——— My——— eyes with love will rest on
dei ne schö——— nen——— Hän - de mir——— die ge - treu - en Au - gen

thee. Be thou——— with——— me,
zu. Bist du——— bei——— mir,

My joy and glad - ness, In deep——— re -
geh' ich mit Freu - den, zum Ster - ben———

pose my soul——— shall——— rest, My——— soul shall rest in deep re - pose.
und zu mei - ner——— Ruh, zum——— Ster - ben und zu mei - ner Ruh'.

Aria
(Willst Du Dein Herz Mir Schenken)

Johann Sebastian Bach

Moderato

Lyrics:

1. Willst du dein Herz mir schen-ken, so fang' es—heim-lich an, daß un-ser bei-der Den-ken nie - mand— er-ra - ten kann. Die Lie - be muß— bei— bei-den all-zeit ver-schwie-gen sein,— drum

schließ die größ - ten Freu - den in dei - nem Her - zen ein.

Additional Lyrics

2. Behutsam sei and schweige, und traue keiner Wand,
   Ließ' innerlich und zeige dich außen unbekannt.
   Kein Argwohn mußt du geben, Verstellung nötig ist,
   Genug, daß du, mein Leben, der Treu' versichert bist.

3. Begehre keine Blicke von meiner Liebe nicht,
   Der Neid hat viele Stücke auf unser Tun gericht't.
   Du mußt die Brust verschließen, hal't' deine Neigung ein,
   Die Lust, die wir genießen, muß ein Geheimnis sein.

4. Zu frei sein, sich ergehen, hat oft Gefahr gebracht,
   Man muß sich wohl verstehen, weil ein falsch Auge wacht.
   Du mußt den Spruch bedenken, den ich zuvor getan;
   Willst du dein Herz mir schenken, so fang es heimlich an.

Ave Maria

Franz Joseph Schubert

Molto lento

A - ve Ma - ri - a! gra - ti - a ple -

na, Ma - ri - a, gra - ti - a ple na, Ma - ri - a, gra - ti - a ple-

na, A - ve,———— A - ve! Do - mi - nus,———— Do-mi-nus— te-cum. Be-ne-

di - cta tu in mu - li-e-ri-bus, et be - ne - di - ctus, et

be - ne - di - ctus fru-ctus ven-tris, ven-tris tu - i, Je - sus.

A - ve Ma - ri - a!

fp

pp

ho - ra mor - tis no - strae,   in   ho - ra mor - tis, mor - tis no - strae,   in

ho - ra mor - tis no - strae.   A   -   ve Ma - ri   -

a!

A   -   ve Ma - ri   -   a!   gra - ti - a____ ple -

na, Ma - ri - a,— gra - ti - a ple - na, Ma - ri - a, gra - ti - a - ple-

na, A - ve, - A - ve! Do-mi - nus,———— Do-mi - nus— tecum; Be - ne -

di - cta tu in mu-li-e- ri bus, et be - ne - di - ctus, et

be - ne - di - ctus fru - ctus ven - tris, ventris tu - i, Je - sus.

A - ve Ma - ri - a!

Ave Maria

Johann Sebastian Bach
adapted by Charles Gounod

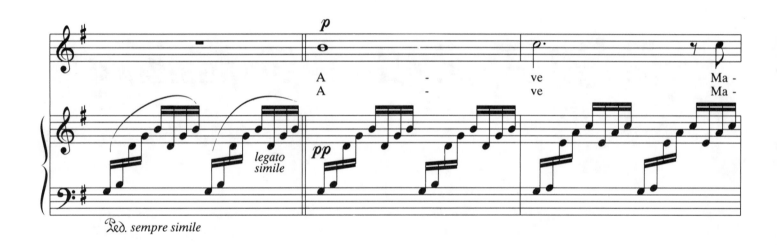

ven- tris_____ cu - i Je - sus._____
son,_____ the son of God, the Lord most high!_____

dim.   p

Sanc - ta Ma - ri - a,
Bless - ed Ma - ri - a!

cresc. molto   f
sanc - ta Ma - ri - a, Ma -
Bless - ed Ma - ri - a! Ma -

cresc. molto

p
ri - a, o - ra pro no - bis,
ri - a! Pray,_____ oh, pray_____ for_____ us,

pp

O Lord Most Holy
(Panis Angelicus)

Cesar Franck

O lov - ing Fa - ther, Thee would we be prais - ing
Dat pa - nis coe - li - cus fi - gu - ris ter - mi -

sempre legato

al - ways. Help us to know — Thee, know Thee and
num. O res mi - ra - bi - lis man - du - cat

sempre legato

love Thee; Fa - ther, Fa - ther, grant us Thy truth and
Do - mi - num, pau - per, pau - per, ser - vus et hu - mi -

grace; Fa - ther, Fa - ther, guide and de - fend —
lis, Pau - per, pau - per, (f)ser - vus et hu - mi -

us.
lis.

Rule   Thou   our   wil - ful   hearts,   Keep   Thee   our
Pa   -   nis   an   -   ge - li - cus   fit   pa   -   nis

wan- d'ring thoughts;   In   all   our   sor - rows let us   find   our   rest   in
ho - mi - num   (f) Dat   pa   -   nis   coe   -   li - cus fi   -   gu - ris ter - mi -

Thee;   And   in   temp -ta- tion's   hour,   Save   through   Thy
num,   O   res   mi - ra - bi - lis   man   -   du - cat

mighty pow'r, Thine aid O send us; Hear
Do - mi - num, *Pau - per,* *pau - per, ser -*

us in mer - cy, Show us Thy
vus et hu - mi - lis *Pau - per,*

fa - vor, So shall we live, and sing praise to Thee.
pau - per, ser - vus ser - vus et hu - mi - lis.

Sarabande

from *Anna Magdalena Notebook*

Johann Sebastian Bach

Sarabande In E Minor

George Frideric Handel

Grave

Sarabande In D Minor

George Frideric Handel

Fanfares

Jean-Joseph Mouret

Allegro vivace

Allegro

William Boyce

Hallelujah Chorus

from *Messiah*

George Frideric Handel

Hornpipe

George Frideric Handel

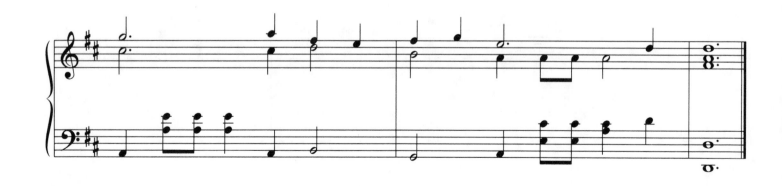

Voluntary On The Doxology (Old 100th)

Henry Purcell

Wedding March

from *A Midsummer Night's Dream*

Felix Mendelssohn

Allegro marcia

Adagio

from *Water Music Suite*

George Frideric Handel

Andante

from *Water Music Suite*

George Frideric Handel

Larghetto

George Frideric Handel

Prelude In C

from *The Well-Tempered Clavier, Part I*

Johann Sebastian Bach